Just Right READING

Level B

D1297906

Options Publishing Inc.

Level B

Acknowledgments

Product Development: The Quarasan Group, Inc.
Cover Design: The Quarasan Group, Inc.
Editor: Amy Gilbert
Production Supervisor: Sandy Batista

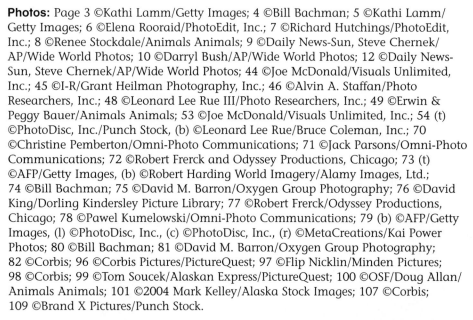

Credits   Abbreviations are as follows: t=top, c=center, b=bottom, l=left, r=right

Photos: Page 3 ©Kathi Lamm/Getty Images; 4 ©Bill Bachman; 5 ©Kathi Lamm/ Getty Images; 6 ©Elena Rooraid/PhotoEdit, Inc.; 7 ©Richard Hutchings/PhotoEdit, Inc.; 8 ©Renee Stockdale/Animals Animals; 9 ©Daily News-Sun, Steve Chernek/ AP/Wide World Photos; 10 ©Darryl Bush/AP/Wide World Photos; 12 ©Daily News-Sun, Steve Chernek/AP/Wide World Photos; 44 ©Joe McDonald/Visuals Unlimited, Inc.; 45 ©I-R/Grant Heilman Photography, Inc.; 46 ©Alvin A. Staffan/Photo Researchers, Inc.; 48 ©Leonard Lee Rue III/Photo Researchers, Inc.; 49 ©Erwin & Peggy Bauer/Animals Animals; 53 ©Joe McDonald/Visuals Unlimited, Inc.; 54 (t) ©PhotoDisc, Inc./Punch Stock, (b) ©Leonard Lee Rue/Bruce Coleman, Inc.; 70 ©Christine Pemberton/Omni-Photo Communications; 71 ©Jack Parsons/Omni-Photo Communications; 72 ©Robert Frerck and Odyssey Productions, Chicago; 73 (t) ©AFP/Getty Images, (b) ©Robert Harding World Imagery/Alamy Images, Ltd.; 74 ©Bill Bachman; 75 ©David M. Barron/Oxygen Group Photography; 76 ©David King/Dorling Kindersley Picture Library; 77 ©Robert Frerck/Odyssey Productions, Chicago; 78 ©Pawel Kumelowski/Omni-Photo Communications; 79 (b) ©AFP/Getty Images, (l) ©PhotoDisc, Inc., (c) ©PhotoDisc, Inc., (r) ©MetaCreations/Kai Power Photos; 80 ©Bill Bachman; 81 ©David M. Barron/Oxygen Group Photography; 82 ©Corbis; 96 ©Corbis Pictures/PictureQuest; 97 ©Flip Nicklin/Minden Pictures; 98 ©Corbis; 99 ©Tom Soucek/Alaskan Express/PictureQuest; 100 ©OSF/Doug Allan/ Animals Animals; 101 ©2004 Mark Kelley/Alaska Stock Images; 107 ©Corbis; 109 ©Brand X Pictures/Punch Stock.

Illustrations: Kathi Ember: 11, 13, 14, 15, 16; Nathan Young Jarvis: 14; Meredith Johnson: 18, 19, 20, 21, 22, 23, 24, 25, 30; Molly Delaney: 31, 32, 33, 34, 35, 36, 38, 39, 40, 41, 42; Jason Wolff: 46, 50, 51, 52, 55, 56; Peter Grosshauser: 57, 58, 59, 60, 61, 62, 63, 64, 66; Kathryn Mitter: 83, 84, 85, 86, 87, 88, 89, 92, 93; Gary R. Phillips: 102, 104, 105, 106

ISBN 1-59137-440-5

Options Publishing Inc.
P.O. Box 1749
Merrimack, NH 03054-1749
TOLL FREE: 800-782-7300 • TOLL FREE FAX: 866-424-4056

www.optionspublishing.com

2

Table of Contents

Lesson 1 Animal Doctors 5

Lesson 2 Ready for the Derby 18

Lesson 3 A Trip to the City 31

Lesson 4 Home, Sweet Home 44

Lesson 5 Oscar's Arms 57

Table of Contents

Lesson 6 Basket Making 70

Lesson 7 No Stamps Needed 83

Lesson 8 Wonderful Whales 96

Review 109

Glossary 111

Get Ready to Read
Animal Doctors

1 Topic

how vets help animals

2 Words to Learn

vet a doctor for animals

cure to make feel better

checkup when a vet checks an animal to see if it is healthy

injured hurt

3 Building Background

What do you know about taking care of animals?

Animal Doctors

A **vet** is a doctor who takes care of animals. Vets are very special people. They work with many kinds of animals.

To become a vet, a person has a lot to learn. Vets have to go to college for six years. They learn about all kinds of animals. Some vets study animals that are pets. Other vets study wild animals. They learn many ways that animals can get sick. They must know how to **cure** them. But most of all, vets must love animals!

A vet looks at a rabbit.

Vets who take care of pets give lots of **checkups**. They make sure the pets stay healthy. Vets listen to the pet's breathing. They check its paws and eyes. Sometimes vets have to give the pets shots. These shots can help keep a pet well.

Many pets do not like to get shots. Some are a bit scared to go to the vet. A good vet can give a shot quickly. It is over before the pet even knows it!

A cat gets a checkup.

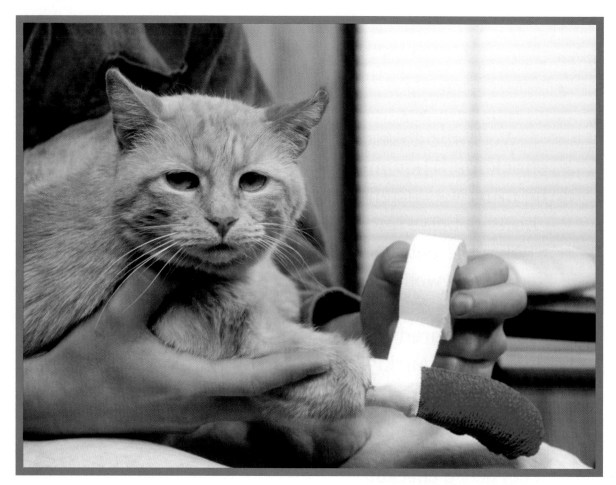

A vet helps an injured cat.

Why do you think a vet must act fast when a pet is hurt?

Sometimes a pet is rushed to a vet because it is **injured**. When this happens, the vet must act fast. She might need to sew up a cut or fix a broken bone. Then she must make sure that the pet does not hurt too much. A sick pet will feel safe with a caring vet. The pet owner will feel better, too.

Some vets will drive a van to help hurt animals. A horse might have a hurt leg or a cut. A vet will bring special things in the van. Vets need to be ready for anything.

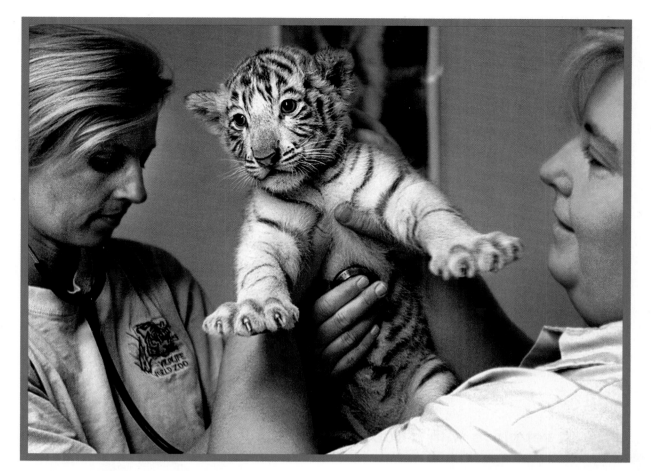

A baby tiger gets a checkup.

Some vets work with animals that are not pets. Animals in zoos, parks, and in the wild get sick, too. Vets help animals, such as dolphins, elephants, or tigers. Animals that do not live with people sometimes need special care. They might be afraid if a person comes close. The vets must be very careful, so they stay safe, too.

How can you tell that this animal is not afraid of the vet?

Being a vet is a very important job. A vet has the chance to work with all kinds of animals. Vets help our animal friends stay healthy. They also take care of hurt animals. Some vets get to work with animals we never see up close. Most vets feel the same about their work. They like their jobs because they have a great love for animals.

A vet plays with a baby elephant.

Main Idea

> The main idea is the most important idea in a story or article.

▶ **What is the article mostly about? Circle the best answer.**

- Vets help wild animals.
- Vets help all kinds of animals.
- Animals sometimes get sick or injured.

▶ **Answer the questions below.**

1 What might be another good title for this article?

_____

_____

2 Why is this a good title?

_____

_____

_____

_____

Main Idea

> The main idea is the most important idea in the story or article. As you read, look for a sentence that tells the main idea.

▶ **Read this part of the article.**

Some vets work with animals that are not pets. Animals in zoos, parks, and in the wild get sick, too. Vets help animals, such as dolphins, elephants, or tigers. Animals that do not live with people sometimes need special care. They might be afraid if a person comes close. The vets must be very careful, so they stay safe, too.

1 Write the sentence that tells the main idea.

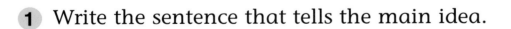

_____

2 Write a title for the paragraph.

_____

_____

More Than One

For many words, you can add s to show more than one.

cat + s = cats

dog + s = dogs

For words that end with s, ss, sh, ch, x, or z, add es to show more than one.

class + es = classes

beach + es = beaches

▶ **Add s or es to these words to show more than one.**

pet _____   peach _____

van _____   class _____

▶ **Add s or es to each word to finish the sentences.**

1 The vet has six bed _____ for pets.

2 Seals like to lay on sunny beach _____ .

3 My mom likes to feed the bird _____ in the backyard.

4 We saw many fox _____ in the woods.

5 Dogs come in many size _____ .

Short *a* and Short *e*

Some words have the short a sound.

tap   The letter a in the word <u>tap</u> has the short a sound.

Some words have the short e sound.

bed   The letter e in the word <u>bed</u> has the short e sound.

head   The word <u>head</u> also has the short e sound.

▶ One of these animals needs help. Draw a line to connect the short e words. They will lead you to the right animal.

wet

log

red

vet   leg

pet

feet

them

fed

web

bread

pen

bag

hen

pig

Words to Learn

| vet | cure | injured | checkup |

▶ **Read the words in the box. Write the word that answers each clue.**

1 This is what you do when you make a sick person feel better. _____

2 I take care of sick animals. _____

3 A vet gives this to make sure your pet is healthy. _____

4 This is what you are if you get hurt.

_____

▶ **Write the correct word to finish each sentence.**

1 After his _____, my rabbit wants to go home. (checkup/vet)

2 My job at the vet's office is to help the animals that have been _____. (cure/injured)

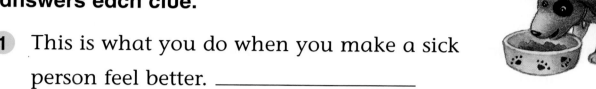

3 Vets love to _____ animals that are sick. (checkup/cure)

4 Our dog got a shot when he went to the _____. (cure/vet)

Reread

Before reading something out loud, look for any hard words. Practice those words. When you know how to say them, read the whole passage out loud.

▶ **Look for any hard words in the passage below. Practice sounding them out. Then take turns with a partner reading the passage out loud.**

Sometimes a pet is rushed to a vet because it is injured. When this happens, the vet must act fast. She might need to sew up a cut or fix a broken bone. Then she must make sure that the pet does not hurt too much. A sick pet will feel safe with a caring vet. The pet owner will feel better, too.

Some vets will drive a van to help hurt animals. A horse might have a hurt leg or a cut. A vet will bring special things in the van. Vets need to be ready for anything.

Some vets work with animals that are not pets. Animals in zoos, parks, and in the wild get sick, too. Vets help animals, such as dolphins, elephants, or tigers. Animals that do not live with people sometimes need special care. They might be afraid if a person comes close. The vets must be very careful, so they stay safe, too.

Extend and Write

▶ **If you were a vet, what kinds of animals would you like to work with? List the animals below. Then write why you would like to work with them.**

The animals I would like to work with:

_____

_____

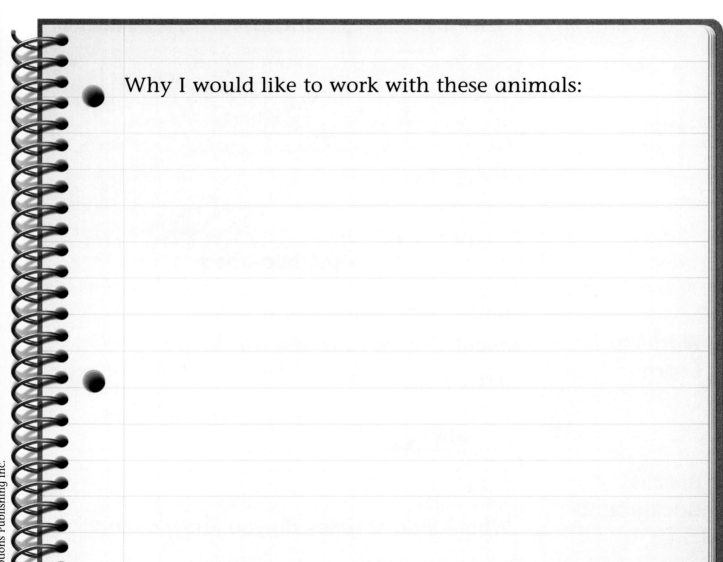

Why I would like to work with these animals:

Get Ready to Read
Ready for the Derby

1 Characters

Pablo
Todd's friend

Todd
Pablo's friend

Cruz
bike shop owner

2 Setting

a neighborhood

3 Words to Learn

ramp a slanted piece of wood

model a small copy of a car

derby a race

workshop a place with tools to build and fix things

4 Building Background

What kinds of races do you know about?

Ready for the Derby

"Quick! Catch the car," Todd gasped. The race car flipped over and off the **ramp**. This was not the first time the **model** had flipped over. What was wrong? The boys had been working on their model for weeks. All of their friends had finished their models.

"The Parker School **Derby** is a week away," said Pablo. "What are we going to do?"

Just then Cruz stopped by. He knew the boys were working on a model for the derby. He asked if they were done yet.

"Hi, Cruz," said Todd. "We are not even close to being done. We can't keep the car from flipping over."

Cruz looked at the car. "The front end is too heavy. These bottle caps also get in the way of the wheels. That will make the car flip over. Bring it over to my **workshop**. We can work on it there."

The boys had never been in the workshop before. That was where Cruz worked on all the bikes. The walls of the workshop were filled with pictures. They showed Cruz winning many races. There was also a bright red model car on a shelf. "Look at this!" Pablo yelled. "Where did you get this model?"

Cruz told them about a day long ago. He had won the Parker School Derby with that model. "I was about as old as you are now," he said with a grin.

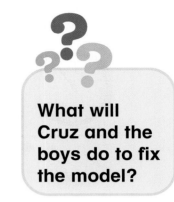

What will Cruz and the boys do to fix the model?

21

How will Cruz's tips help the boys?

The three worked in the shop all day. "Wait a minute!" said Todd. "Don't throw away my bottle caps! They make the car look cool."

"The bottle caps hit the wheels," said Cruz. "That's why it flips over."

Now the front of the car came to a point. It was clean and smooth. Cruz brought out some paint. "Can we paint the model red just like yours?" asked Pablo.

Cruz smiled. "Sure," he said.

22

The boys were ready for the derby at last.
In practice the model had not tipped over once.
Todd and Pablo waited at the top of the ramp.
The race started and the cars rolled down the
ramp. They were all going very fast. At the last
second, the bright red car pulled ahead. It
raced across the finish line! Todd, Pablo, and
Cruz gave each other high-fives. They yelled,
"WE WON!" With Cruz's help, the boys had
won the derby.

Making Predictions

To predict means to guess what will happen next. As you read, think about what might happen next, and make a prediction.

▶ **Read the sentences. Circle the sentence that tells what might happen at the next Parker School Derby.**

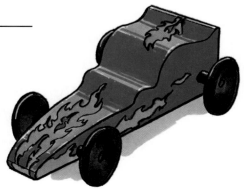

Cruz will help the boys with their model again.

Todd will glue his flags back onto the model.

The boys will not want to race model cars again.

▶ **Write sentences to tell why you think this might happen.**

_____

_____

_____

_____

_____

Making Predictions

▶ **Read the paragraph. Then write what you predict will happen next. Tell why you think that might happen.**

Pablo and Todd went by Cruz's Bike Shop. Cruz was in the workshop in the back. He was working on a new bike. "What is the bike for, Cruz?" asked Todd.

"I am racing next week," Cruz said. "Now all I need are two teammates. They need to be at the race to help me if I get a flat tire. They also carry bottles of water and snacks I can eat as I ride."

Todd and Pablo looked at each other. Then they both grinned.

_____

_____

_____

_____

_____

_____

_____

Verb Endings

A verb is an action word. Add **s** to some verbs to show that one person or thing is doing an action now.

run + **s** = runs

The race car runs down the ramp.

Add **ed** to verbs to show that an action has already happened.

work + **ed** = worked

Last week, the boys worked on the car.

▶ **Add s or ed to each word to make the sentences correct.**

1 Last night, Todd spill_____ some paint on the floor.

2 Pablo run_____ to catch the car.

3 Yesterday Cruz roll_____ the car down the ramp.

▶ **Add s or ed to the words in the story below.**

"Let's see if the car tip_____ over now," said Cruz. The boys wait_____ while Cruz set up a ramp in his shop. Then they tried the new car. The little red car rush_____ down the ramp. "Wow!" said Todd. This car run_____ great."

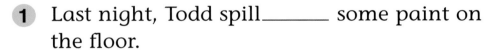

Short *i*, *o*, and *u*

> grin   The letter i in <u>grin</u> has the **short i** sound.
>
> shop   The letter o in <u>shop</u> has the **short o** sound.
>
> run   The letter u in <u>run</u> has the **short u** sound.

▶ **Read the words in the word box.**

tip	fun	got	sit	tug	top	win	job	up

▶ **Write a word with the short i sound to finish each sentence.**

1 The boys want to _____ the car race.

2 Cruz will _____ by the finish line.

▶ **Write a word with the short o sound to finish each sentence.**

1 Cruz _____ out some red paint.

2 Todd might want a _____ at the bike shop.

▶ **Write a word with the short u sound to finish each sentence.**

1 Cruz had to _____ on the bottle caps to get them off the model car.

2 The boys had _____ making the model.

Words to Learn

derby	workshop	ramp	model

▶ **Write the correct word from the word box to finish each sentence.**

1 Todd plans to make a blue _____ for the next race.

2 The boys fixed the model using tools in Cruz's _____.

3 The _____ at the school looked as tall as a cliff.

4 The whole neighborhood raced cars in the _____.

▶ **Write the correct word from the word box to finish each sentence.**

1 She had never raced a _____ in the derby before.

2 We built a _____ to race our models on.

3 Please put the tools in the _____, where they belong.

4 We will have to work hard if we want to win first place in the _____ this year.

Reread

Quotation marks come before and after what someone says. When you see quotation marks, you know someone is speaking. Make sure to read each character's speech with feeling.

▶ **Underline what each character says in the passage below. Read the passage aloud to a partner. Then switch.**

Cruz looked at the car. "The front end is too heavy. These bottle caps also get in the way of the wheels. That will make the car flip over. Bring it over to my workshop. We can work on it there."

The boys had never been in the workshop before. That was where Cruz worked on all the bikes. The walls of the workshop were filled with pictures. They showed Cruz winning many races. There was also a bright red model car on a shelf. "Look at this!" Pablo yelled. "Where did you get this model?"

Cruz told them about a day long ago. He had won the Parker School Derby with that model. "I was about as old as you are now," he said with a grin.

Extend and Write

▶ Imagine you could enter the Parker School
Derby. Describe what your car would look like.
Draw a picture of it.

_____

_____

_____

_____

_____

_____

_____

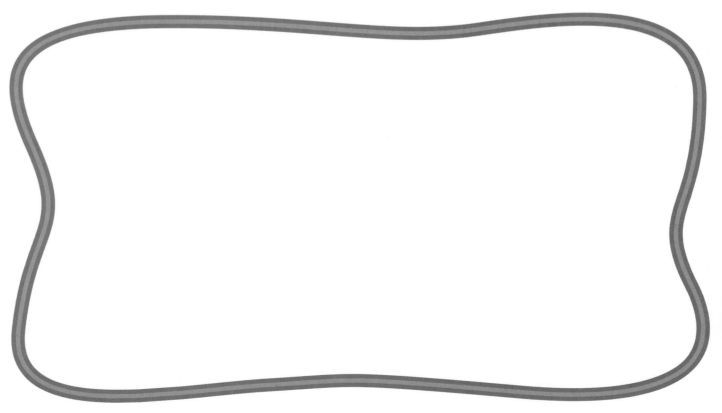

Get Ready to Read
A Trip to the City

1 Characters

Mom
James's
mother

James
her son

conductor
a worker on
the train

2 Setting

the city

3 Words to Learn

market a place where things are sold

conductor a person who works on a train

parade an event where people gather to watch other people march down a street

display to show off paintings or drawings

4 Building Background

- **Have you been to a market?**
- **What did you do there?**

A Trip to the City

Mom and I were going into the city for the day. She said she wanted to take me to the street **market**. I was excited about the train ride. But I was not excited about going to the street market. Who wants to see a bunch of fruits and vegetables? Mom told me I would be surprised.

The **conductor** asked me, "Where are you headed today?"

"We are going to the street market," I said.

"Well, you'll see the **parade** on your way. There's also an art fair," said the conductor.

"A parade!" I cried. "I love parades."

We got off the train. We could see the parade in the distance.

"Hurry, Mom!" I said.

We found a spot to watch the parade. There was a huge marching band on the street. They were all dressed in the same bright clothes. They all marched to the beat of the drums.

Mom and I watched the band march down the street. I told Mom that I wanted to play the drums in a marching band.

Why does James love parades?

What did James enjoy about the art fair?

Then, I saw some artwork. Many artists had paintings or drawings on **display**. We went to get a better look.

Along the way, I saw a man drawing a young girl's picture. I had an idea. "Mom, let's ask him to draw our picture, so we can remember this trip to the city," I said.

"That's a great idea, James," said Mom.

So we sat together as the man drew our picture. I was surprised by how quickly he finished the drawing.

We left the art fair and walked to the street market. It had so much more than just fruits and vegetables. "Let's look here," Mom said.

"Wow!" I exclaimed. A man was selling baseball cards in his booth. My mom got me a card of my favorite player.

We moved on to other booths. We saw one with colorful baskets. Another one had T-shirts. We even saw one with wooden masks.

By the end of the street market, I was hungry. So I was glad that they had fruit there, too!

When it was time to go home, we went back to the train station. The same conductor was still working. I was excited to see him. "Well? How was your day?" he asked.

"We did so many things!" I said. I told the conductor about the marching band. I showed him the drawing of Mom and me. I even told him how much I liked the street market.

The conductor smiled and went back to work. Mom asked, "So what did you think about the city?"

"It was full of surprises! Thanks, Mom."

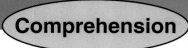
Drawing Conclusions

Sometimes an author doesn't tell you everything that happens in a story. Use what you know from the story to figure out what happens.

▶ **Read the sentences. Then write your answers on the lines.**

1 The conductor told James and his mom about the parade and the art fair. Later, he asked them how their day went.

What do you know about the conductor?

_____

2 James saw the parade in the distance. He asked his mom to hurry.

Why was James in a hurry?

_____

3 James said "Wow!" when he saw all of the baseball cards.

What does James think about baseball cards?

_____

4 James said he was hungry at the end of the day.

What did James eat?

_____

Drawing Conclusions

▶ **Read each paragraph. Write a sentence to answer each question.**

I showed the baseball card to my friends. They thought it was really cool. I decided to save some money so I could collect more cards of my favorite team. Then I asked Mom if we could go back to the street market.

1 How did James feel about his baseball card?

_____

2 Why did James want to go back to the street market? _____

Mom took me back to the street market. When we got to the booth where the baseball cards had been, they were gone! The booth was full of pots and mugs. "That's okay, James," said Mom. "Maybe we can find them somewhere else." But as we walked along, I saw a man selling small drums. So I spent my money after all!

3 How did James feel when he saw that the baseball cards were gone?

_____

4 What did James buy with his money?

_____

Contractions

Words such as <u>can't</u>, <u>didn't</u>, and <u>I'll</u> are contractions. A contraction is a shorter form of two words put together. An apostrophe (') shows that one or more letters are missing.

can + not = can't
did + not = didn't
I + will = I'll

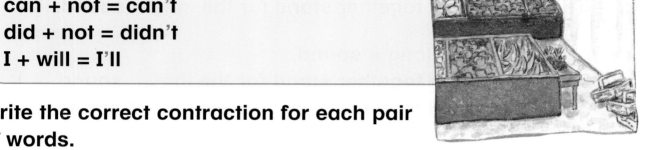

▶ **Write the correct contraction for each pair of words.**

1 we will _____   **4** I have _____

2 you are _____   **5** he is _____

3 is not _____   **6** you will _____

▶ **Rewrite the sentences. Make two words from each sentence into a contraction.**

1 Mom said, "We will go back to the street market again."

_____

2 I hope that she is going to buy me another baseball card.

_____

3 The market is not just full of fruits and vegetables.

_____

Long *a* and Long *e*

Some words have the long a sound.

cave   The letter e at the end of the word makes the a
       stand for the long a sound.

pail   The a and the i together stand for the long a sound.

hay   The a and the y together stand for the long a sound.

Some words have the long e sound.

sleep The e and the e together stand for the long e sound.

beat   The e and the a together stand for the long e sound.

▶ **Read the riddles. Answer the riddles with words from the box.**

face	rail	day	seat	sleep	play

1 This is when the sun is up. It rhymes with
"say." _____

2 When you ride on a train, you sit on this.
It rhymes with "meet." _____

3 This is when you dream. It rhymes with
"creep." _____

4 It is fun to do this. It rhymes with "bay." _____

5 A train rides on this. It rhymes with "pail." _____

6 This is the front part of your head.
It rhymes with "pace." _____

Words to Learn

market	conductor	parade	display

▶ **Write a word from the box to finish each sentence.**

1 There were many people marching in the _____.

2 The paintings were on _____ on the wall.

3 You can buy many different things at a _____.

4 I hope I can work as a train _____ when I grow up.

▶ **Write the correct words from the box to complete the paragraph.**

On Saturday, we took a train to visit my Grandma and Grandpa. We said "hi" to the _____ as we got on the train. When we got off the train, we saw posters on _____. The posters told about a _____ with marching bands. We all went to the parade. Then we stopped at the _____ to buy corn on the cob. It was so much fun!

Reread

When you read aloud, notice how each sentence
ends. Remember, when you read a sentence with
a question mark, make your voice go up at the
end of the sentence. When you read a sentence
that ends with an exclamation point, make your
voice sound excited.

▶ Circle the question marks and exclamation
points in the passage below. With a partner,
take turns reading this part of the story aloud.
Remember to use your voice to show the
meaning of each sentence.

   The conductor asked me, "Where are you
headed today?"

   "We are going to the street market," I said.

   "Well, you'll see the parade on your way.
There's also an art fair," said the conductor.

   "A parade!" I cried. "I love parades."

   We got off the train. We could see the
parade in the distance.

   "Hurry, Mom!" I said.

Extend and Write

▶ James and his mom saw a parade, an art fair, and a street market. Write about which one you would enjoy the most. Tell why you think you would like it.

4

Get Ready to Read
Home, Sweet Home

groundhogs

1 Topic

2 Words to Learn

groundhogs small animals that dig holes and sleep through most of the winter

gnaw chew

dens homes under the ground where some animals live

bulldozers big tractors that dig and move dirt

3 Building Background

- **What do you know about groundhogs?**

- **What do you think you will read about groundhogs in this article?**

Home, Sweet Home

What do you know about **groundhogs**? Groundhogs are small animals with brown fur. They have short, bushy tails and strong legs. Groundhogs have special ears. Their ears can open and close! Groundhogs close their ears when they dig. This keeps the dirt out of their ears. Groundhogs are also called woodchucks. They have special teeth that never stop growing! Groundhogs have to **gnaw** on things so their teeth do not grow too long.

Groundhogs' teeth never stop growing.

How are groundhogs like bulldozers?

Groundhogs make good homes. They are very good at digging. They look for fields or other open places close to grass and other plants. Then the groundhogs dig their **dens**. Their strong legs help them dig deep into the ground. With their strong teeth, they break rocks into pieces. Groundhogs push the dirt out of the dens with their heads. Groundhogs are like **bulldozers**. Watch the dirt fly!

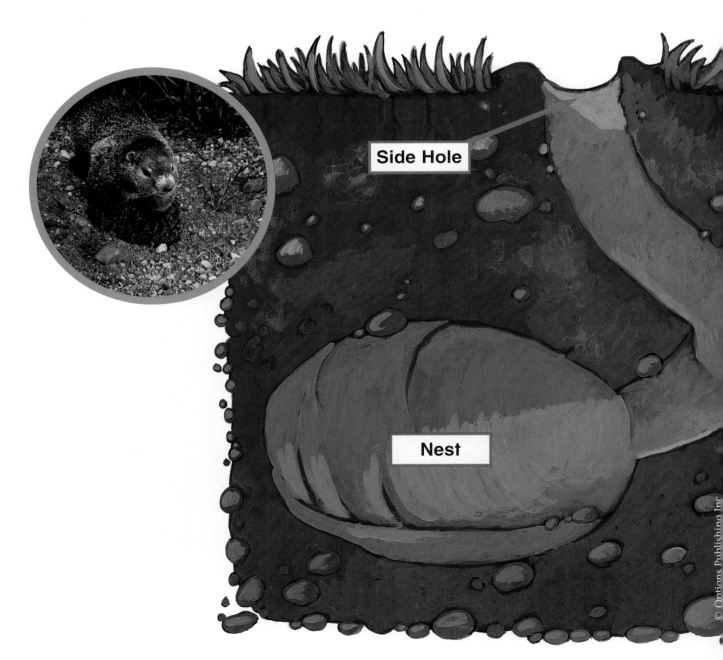

Side Hole

Nest

Groundhog dens have more than one hole. Groundhogs go in and out of the holes. They hide one of the holes from other animals. This helps keep the groundhogs safe. Groundhogs also dig tunnels. The tunnels all go to the dens.

Groundhogs sleep in their dens. They build a nest in the room where they sleep. Groundhogs line their nests with dry grass so they can stay warm.

Why do you think groundhogs dig more than one hole to their dens?

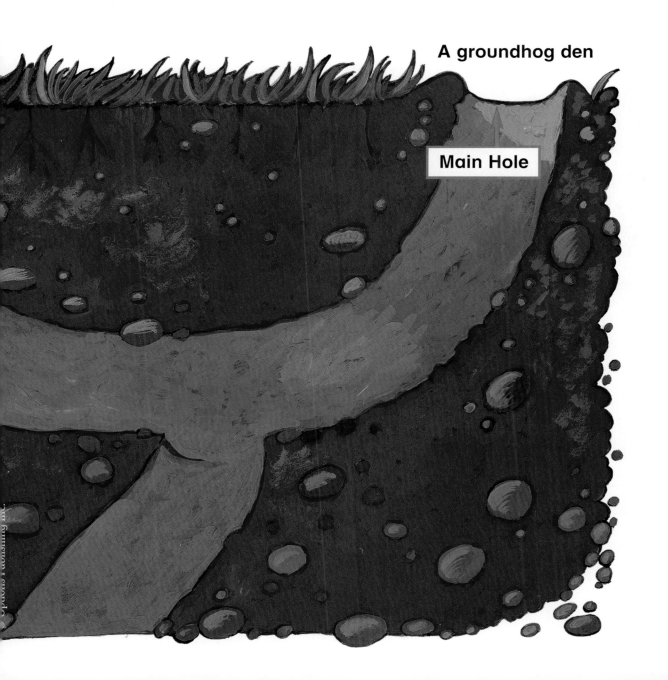

A groundhog den

Main Hole

Groundhogs dig one den for summer and another den for winter. In the summer, groundhogs like to be outside. They love resting on warm rocks on sunny days.

Groundhogs also love to eat! They eat grass and other plants. Groundhogs need to eat a lot before winter comes. In the winter, groundhogs go into their dens for a deep sleep.

A groundhog resting in the sun

When winter comes, groundhogs go to new dens. Their winter dens are in forests. The ground there does not get as cold as the ground in fields. Sometimes other animals move into the old dens. Groundhogs don't mind. They are too busy sleeping! Groundhogs sleep with their tails around them like blankets. They wake up about once a month because they need to eat.

On February 2nd, we have Groundhog Day. But most groundhogs stay asleep in their dens until spring comes. Then they leave their dens. It's time for more digging, resting, and eating!

A groundhog eating plants

Cause and Effect

Sometimes one thing makes another thing happen. Read this sentence.

In winter, groundhogs wake up once a month because they need to eat.

What Happens = Groundhogs wake up.
Why = They need to eat.

▶ Draw a line to finish each sentence.
Match what happens with why it happens.
The first one has been done for you.

What Happens

1 Groundhogs rest on rocks in the sun •

2 Groundhogs chew on things •

3 Groundhogs eat a lot in the summer •

4 Groundhogs dig tunnels •

Why

• because the rocks are warm.

• because they sleep most of the winter.

• because they need to get to their dens.

• because they need to keep their teeth short.

© Options Publishing Inc.

Cause and Effect

▶ **Fill in the chart by writing what happens. The first one has been done for you.**

Why   **What Happens**

1 Groundhogs don't want dirt in their ears → so they close their ears.

2 Groundhogs line their nests with dry grass → so they can _____ _____ _____.

3 Groundhogs hide one of the holes from other animals → because _____ _____ _____.

4 Groundhogs go to new dens in the winter → because _____ _____ _____.

Compound Words

> In a compound word, two words are put together
> to make a new word. Look at the example.
>
> **ground + hog = groundhog**

▶ **Put together each pair of words below.
Write the compound word you make.**

1 out + side = _____

2 sun + shine = _____

3 grand + mother = _____

4 wood + chucks = _____

5 back + yard = _____

▶ **Use the compound words you made to finish
the sentences below.**

1 My _____ gave me a groundhog book.

2 Another name for groundhogs is _____.

3 Groundhogs would like the grass in our

_____.

4 Do groundhogs like to sleep _____
when it is cold?

5 Groundhogs love to rest on rocks in the

warm _____.

© Options Publishing Inc.

Long *i* and Long *o*

hide	The letter e at the end of this word makes the i stand for the long i sound.
pie	The letters i and e together stand for the long i sound.
hole	The letter e at the end of this word makes the o stand for the long o sound.
coat	The letters o and a together stand for the long o sound.

hide	log	road	line	dig
holes	rock	fit	home	lie

▶ **Write words with the long o sound to finish the sentences.**

1 A den is a groundhog's _____.

2 A groundhog den can have many _____.

3 A tunnel is a _____ under the ground.

▶ **Write words with the long i sound to finish the sentences.**

1 Groundhogs like to _____ on warm rocks in the sun.

2 Groundhogs _____ in their dens.

3 Groundhogs _____ their nests with dry grass.

Words to Learn

groundhogs	dens	bulldozers	gnaw

▶ **Use the words in the box to answer the riddles.**

1 They are very big and can dig a lot of dirt. _____

2 They are homes under the ground. _____

3 This is what some animals do when they chew. _____

4 They sleep through the winter. _____

▶ **Use the words in the box to finish the sentences.**

1 Woodchucks are also called _____.

2 Woodchucks _____ on things to keep their teeth short.

3 Woodchucks make _____ where they live and sleep.

4 Woodchucks can push dirt with their heads like _____.

Reread

Before reading something out loud, look for any hard words. Practice those words. When you know how to say them, read the whole passage out loud.

▶ **Look for any hard words in the passage below. Practice those words. Then read the passage out loud.**

Groundhogs make good homes. They are very good at digging. They look for fields or other open places close to grass and other plants. Then the groundhogs dig their dens. Their strong legs help them dig deep into the ground. With their strong teeth, they break rocks into pieces. Groundhogs push the dirt out of the dens with their heads. Groundhogs are like bulldozers. Watch the dirt fly!

Extend and Write

▶ **What could you tell a friend about groundhogs? Write your ideas. Then, write a letter to your friend telling three things you learned.**

ideas

_____

_____

_____

_____

February 2, 20_____

Dear _____,

    Do you know what today is? Here is a clue.

Fun Facts About Groundhogs

Groundhogs _____

_____.

Groundhogs _____

_____.

Groundhogs _____

_____.

Happy Groundhog Day!

Your friend,

_____

5

Get Ready to Read
Oscar's Arms

1 Characters

Oscar
an octopus

Craig
a crab

Shannon
a shark

2 Setting

underwater cave

3 Words to Learn

octopus a sea animal with eight arms

excited happy that something is happening

practice to do something many times

startled scared by something

4 Building Background

What kinds of things do you have to practice?

Oscar's Arms

Oscar **Octopus** was very **excited** this morning. Once a week, Craig Crab and Shannon Shark cooked dinner for all of their fish friends. This week it was Oscar's turn to help them cook. Oscar had never cooked before. He knew that Craig and Shannon always made great meals. So Oscar was happy he could help them. Oscar was sure that his eight arms would help Craig and Shannon cook eight times faster. Oscar held his head up high as he got to Craig's cave.

As the friends cooked, all of Oscar's arms kept getting in the way. Shannon asked Oscar, "Will you please pass me a big bowl?"

"Sure!" said Oscar. But as he turned, one of Oscar's arms knocked Craig's cans to the floor. Oscar's face turned red. "I'm so sorry," he said. He quickly picked up the cans.

Craig replied, "Don't worry about it. They are only cans."

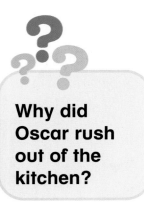

Why did Oscar rush out of the kitchen?

Oscar kept knocking things over. He felt as if he and his eight arms were making his friends cook eight times slower! "I'm not very good at cooking," said Oscar sadly.

Craig replied, "Don't be silly. You just need more **practice** to get better."

Just then the buzzer on the oven went off. The sound **startled** Oscar. He quickly turned. As he turned, one of his arms knocked Craig off the counter.

Oscar rushed out of the kitchen.

Oscar sat at the table with his head hung low. "I'm sorry, Craig. I did not mean to knock you over," said Oscar.

Craig replied, "It's okay. I know you didn't mean it."

"I'm just no good at cooking," mumbled Oscar.

"Don't say that! It takes time to learn something new," replied Craig.

Then Craig began to set the table. He had a hard time with the heavy plates. "Here, let me help," said Oscar. Using all eight of his arms, Oscar set the table in no time. Craig's face lit up with a smile.

Why do you think Craig smiled?

All of the fish friends sat at the table. "I'd like to thank Oscar for being this week's helper," Shannon said.

"Hurray for Oscar!" yelled the fish friends.

"Now Oscar would like to serve you all," Shannon added. Quickly, Oscar's arms went to work. In a flash, Oscar had filled their plates with food. All of the fish friends cheered and then started eating.

Craig leaned over and said to Oscar, "And there are some things that you are good at without having to practice!" Oscar just smiled. He had to agree.

Making Inferences

Sometimes a writer does not tell you everything in a story. When that happens, you have to use clues from the story and what you already know to figure it out.

▶ **Read the questions below. Then circle the best answer to each question.**

1 What do you think the fish friends had for dinner?

- seaweed pie
- hot dogs and hamburgers
- chicken noodle soup

2 Why was Craig having a hard time with the plates?

- He hurt one of his legs while cooking.
- He is lazy and didn't want to set the table.
- He is a lot smaller than the plates.

3 What else might Oscar be good at doing?

- baking a cake
- cleaning the house
- sewing

Making Inferences

▶ **Read these paragraphs. Then answer the questions.**

After dinner, Oscar cleared the dishes from the table in a flash. At the same time, he gave Shannon Shark and Craig Crab a big hug. Craig's eyes got wide and his face turned blue. Oscar quickly let him go. "I'm sorry!" yelled Oscar.

"It's okay," said Craig. Then Oscar proudly began washing the dishes. Craig and Shannon looked at each other and smiled.

1 How could Oscar hug both Shannon and Craig and clear the dishes at the same time?

_____

_____

2 Why do you think Craig's eyes got wide and his face turned blue?

_____

_____

3 Will Oscar be good at washing the dishes? Why or why not?

_____

_____

Who Owns It?

> Add 's to a word to show that something belongs to one person or thing.
>
> claw that belongs to a cat = cat's claw

▶ **Rewrite the phrases using 's.**

1 bark that belongs to the dog

_____

2 bowl that belongs to the fish

_____

3 nest that belongs to the bird

_____

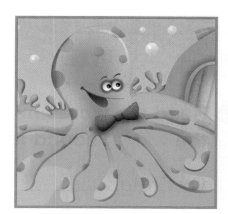

▶ **Replace the underlined words using a phrase with 's.**

1 The shell that belongs to Craig is hard so his back will not get hurt.

_____

2 The arms that belong to Oscar are long and allow him to grab many things.

_____

3 The teeth that belong to Shannon are sharp.

_____

Long *u* and Vowel *y*

cute	The letter e at the end of the word <u>cute</u> makes the u have the long u sound.
heavy	The letter y at the end of the word <u>heavy</u> has the long e sound.
fly	The letter y at the end of <u>fly</u> has the long i sound.

rude	by	many	rule	try	happy

▶ **Read the words in the box. Write words with the long u sound to finish the sentences.**

1 Craig's _____ is "Have fun!"

2 It would be _____ of Oscar if he did not help with the dinner.

▶ **Write words from the box that have the long e sound spelled with a y to finish the sentences.**

1 Oscar felt _____ when he helped.

2 Oscar has _____ arms.

▶ **Write words from the box that have the long i sound spelled with a y to finish the sentences.**

1 Oscar will _____ again.

2 The dining room is _____ the kitchen.

Words to Learn

| octopus | excited | practice | startled |

▶ **Read each meaning. Then write the correct word.**

1 scared by something: _____

2 to do something
many times: _____

3 a sea animal with
eight arms: _____

4 happy that something
is happening: _____

▶ **Write the correct words from the box to complete the passage.**

Although Shannon was a friend, Oscar was a little afraid of her teeth. When Shannon bit down hard on her food, it _____ Oscar.

Then later in the day, Craig said that he needed some extra arms to help him make the dessert. Oscar was _____ because he knew he could help. Since he was an _____, he had eight arms that he could use to help Craig. Also, he would have a chance to _____ making dessert.

Reread

When you read aloud, you should notice certain words that tell you how the character feels. Sometimes a word is placed before or after a speaker's name. That word gives you a clue about how to read what the character says.

▶ With a partner, take turns reading this part of the story aloud. Remember to use your voice to show how a character feels as he speaks.

Oscar sat at the table with his head hung low. "I'm sorry, Craig. I did not mean to knock you over," said Oscar.

Craig replied, "It's okay. I know you didn't mean it."

"I'm just no good at cooking," mumbled Oscar.

"Don't say that! It takes time to learn something new," replied Craig.

Then Craig began to set the table. He had a hard time with the heavy plates. "Here, let me help," said Oscar. Using all eight of his arms, Oscar set the table in no time. Craig's face lit up with a smile.

Extend and Write

▶ **What kinds of meals do you think Shannon and Craig make? What would they cook for each of their fish friends? Write about the food and what is in it.**

Food: _____

What the food is and what is in it:

_____

_____

_____

_____

_____

_____

_____

_____

_____

_____

_____

_____

_____

_____

_____

_____

Get Ready to Read
Basket Making

1 Topic

making baskets

2 Words to Learn

tradition something that has been passed down from parents to children

dye to add bright colors to something

coil to turn a rope in a circle

sew to tie together with a needle and thread

3 Building Background

How do you use baskets?

Basket Making

Baskets have been made and used for many years. Long ago, people used baskets to hold and carry food. Mothers and fathers helped children learn how to make baskets.

Making baskets is still a **tradition**. People make many different kinds of baskets. They use the baskets in different ways.

Basket making

71

Baskets come in many sizes and shapes.

How are baskets used?

Many people use baskets to hold things. But baskets can be used to do jobs, too. Some small baskets are used for cleaning rice. Other big baskets are used to catch fish. Large, strong baskets can hold heavy things.

What are baskets made of?

Most baskets are made of things that come from plants. Often, people use grass and leaves to make rope. Then this rope is used to make the baskets. Some of the other things people use to make baskets are sticks, twigs, and tree bark.

Most baskets are the same color as the plants that were used to make them. But sometimes people want to make baskets that are a different color than the plant. They use a **dye** to color the plants. Dyes can make baskets have bright colors.

How are baskets made?

Many baskets are made by coiling. There are five main steps to coiling a basket.

Step 1 Put the grass or leaves in water. Dry grass and leaves break. Wet grass and leaves are easy to bend. Basket materials must stay wet.

Why must basket materials stay wet?

73

Basket makers make a circle for the bottom of a basket.

Why can't someone sew the ropes together first?

Step 2 Make ropes from the wet grass or leaves. These ropes are used to form the baskets.

Step 3 **Coil** the ropes to make a circle.

Step 4 **Sew** the ropes together. Each circle becomes the bottom of a basket.

Step 5 Build up the sides of the basket. Coil one rope on top of the other. Then sew the ropes together.

As the ropes are coiled on top of one another, the basket gets deeper. What a basket is used for might depend on how deep it is. Once the last coil is put in place, the baskets can be put to work.

The tradition of basket making is still passed down from mothers and fathers to their children. Baskets can be made by hand or with a machine. Many baskets we use today are just like baskets made long ago.

A mother and daughter carry baskets.

Sequence

It is important to follow the steps in a process if you want to do something the right way.

▶ Write the missing steps to make a coiled basket.

Step 1   Put the grass or leaves in water.

Step 2 _____

_____

Step 3 _____

_____

Step 4   Sew the ropes together.

Step 5 _____

_____

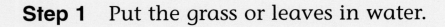

Sequence

▶ **Read the steps that tell how to dye a basket.**

Step 1   Mix the dye and salt into a pot of hot water.

Step 2   Coil the ropes loosely into the water.

Step 3   Leave the ropes in until they are the color you want.

Step 4   Remove the ropes and rinse them with cool water.

Step 5   Hang the ropes to let them dry.

▶ **The following steps are out of order. Write a number next to each step to place the steps in the right order.**

_____ Leave the ropes in until they are the color you want.

_____ Hang the ropes to let them dry.

_____ Mix the dye and salt into a pot of hot water.

_____ Coil the ropes loosely into the water.

_____ Remove the ropes and rinse them with cool water.

Same and Opposite

Some words mean the same or almost the same as other words. The words <u>large</u> and <u>big</u> mean the same thing.

Opposites are words with meanings that are different in every way. The words <u>large</u> and <u>small</u> are opposites.

▶ **Read each sentence. Write a word from the box that means the same as each underlined word.**

loud   pretty   bright

1 We saw some <u>beautiful</u> baskets. _____

2 The people in the market were <u>noisy</u>. _____

3 The baskets looked very <u>colorful</u>. _____

▶ **Read each sentence. Write a word from the box that is the opposite of each underlined word.**

hot   heavy   long

1 We want to carry <u>light</u> things in our basket. _____

2 We used <u>short</u> ropes to coil the basket. _____

3 We mixed the dye in <u>cold</u> water. _____

Beginning Blends

Many words begin with two consonants. Their sounds blend together, but each sound is heard. In the article, you read many words with blends.

grass   dry   step   plants   break   cleaning

clean	stop	step	bread	stick
class	brain	broom	clap	

▶ Write each word from the box under the picture whose name begins with the same blend.

_____   _____   _____

_____   _____   _____

_____   _____   _____

▶ Write a word from the box to complete each sentence.

1 Our _____ is making baskets.

2 The first _____ is to put the materials in water.

3 Some people put _____ in baskets.

Words to Learn

▶ **Answer each clue with a word from the box. Use your answers to fill in the puzzles.**

tradition	dye	coil	sew

Clues

1 to add bright colors to something

_____

2 to tie together with a tiny thread

_____

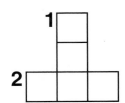

3 to turn around in a circle

4 _____

something passed on from parent to child _____

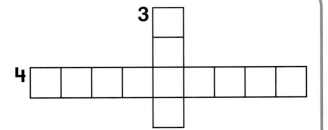

▶ **Name a tradition you know about.**

_____

_____

Reread

Before reading something out loud, look for any hard words or words you don't know. Practice those words. When you know them, read the whole passage out loud.

▶ **Practice any hard words in the passage below. Then read the passage out loud.**

Baskets have been made and used for many years. Long ago, people used baskets to hold and carry food. Mothers and fathers helped children learn how to make baskets.

Making baskets is still a tradition. People make many different kinds of baskets. They use the baskets in different ways.

How are baskets used?

Many people use baskets to hold things. But baskets can be used to do jobs, too. Some small baskets are used for cleaning rice. Other big baskets are used to catch fish. Large, strong baskets can hold heavy things.

Extend and Write

▶ **The article tells you how to make a basket. What else do you know how to make? Write steps to tell someone how to make it.**

How To Make _____

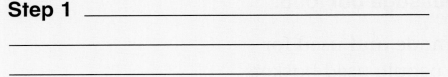

Step 1 _____
_____
_____

Step 2 _____
_____
_____

Step 3 _____
_____
_____

Step 4 _____
_____
_____

Step 5 _____
_____
_____

Get Ready to Read
No Stamps Needed

1 **Characters**

Ella
Nana's
granddaughter

Nana
Ella's
grandmother

2 **Setting**

Ella's house

3 **Words to Learn**

office a room with a desk and a computer where work is done

computer a machine that people use to do many jobs, such as writing letters

e-mail a letter sent from one computer to another

scan to copy a picture onto a computer

4 **Building Background**

How does sending e-mails help people?

No Stamps Needed

On most days, Nana is waiting for me at the door after school. She stays with me until my parents get home. She helps me with my homework.

Today, I found Nana at the kitchen table. She was looking through her bag. I gave her a hug. "I'm out of stamps, Ella," she said. "Can you find me one? I want to send a letter to your cousin Tyson."

I looked in Mom's stamp box in the kitchen. The box was empty. Then I ran to Dad's **office**. Sometimes, he puts stamps in his desk. But I couldn't find one there.

The **computer** was on. So, I stopped for a minute to check my **e-mail**. That gave me an idea. Usually Nana is the one helping me. But maybe I could help her this time.

How do you think Ella will help Nana?

I went back to the kitchen. "I don't have a stamp, but why don't you send Tyson an e-mail?" I asked Nana.

"Well, I thought of that. But I wanted to send him pictures from my vacation. I can't send him the pictures if I e-mail him," she said.

"You can, Nana," I said. "We'll **scan** them into the computer and send them."

Nana followed me to the office. My e-mail center was still on my computer screen. I pushed the WRITE button. An empty e-mail came up on the screen. "First, type the e-mail to Tyson," I said.

Together, Nana and I wrote an e-mail to Tyson. When we finished, Nana said, "Now let's send some pictures."

I scanned the pictures into the computer and they popped up on the computer screen. I showed her how to attach the pictures to the e-mail. "Now click the SEND button," I said. She did, and the e-mail was sent.

"Well!" said Nana. "That was easy!" Nana smiled. "How long will it take?" she asked.

"Not long," I said. Then Nana wanted to send the pictures to Uncle Fred, too.

How does Nana feel about using e-mail to send pictures now?

Nana finished the e-mail to Uncle Fred and attached the pictures herself. "This is so simple," Nana said. "I wish I had learned this sooner!"

Just then, my computer beeped. A new e-mail came up on screen. Nana grinned. "It's a message from Tyson," she said. She read Tyson's message. Best of all, Tyson sent pictures to us from his last baseball game. "I was so sad to miss that game," Nana said. "Sending pictures is great. I can't believe how fast and easy it is. And no stamps needed!"

Understanding Characters

> **You can learn about characters from what they say and do.**

▶ **You got to know Ella and Nana in this story. Think about the things they did. Think about what they said.**

Ella

Nana

▶ **Read the following sentences. Identify who said each sentence. Write the name of the person who did or said the sentence.**

1 "I don't have a stamp, but why don't you send Tyson an e-mail?" _____

2 "I can't send him the pictures if I e-mail him." _____

3 She scanned the pictures into the computer. _____

4 She typed the e-mail to Tyson. _____

5 She learned how to do something new with e-mail. _____

6 In the end, she was happy that she could help someone who has always helped her. _____

Understanding Characters

▶ **Circle the correct ending to each sentence. Then write what you learned about the character from this action. The first one is done for you.**

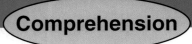

1 Nana stays with Ella after school.
She helps Ella
  • with her schoolwork.
  • make breakfast.

This shows that Nana loves Ella and wants to help .

2 Ella could not find a stamp in the stamp box.
So Ella looked
  • in the kitchen.
  • in her father's desk.

This shows that Ella _____.

3 Ella didn't find a stamp.
But Ella got an idea to
  • show Nana how to send pictures
    using e-mail.
  • make a stamp for the letter.

This shows that Ella _____.

▶ **Tell how Nana changed by the end of the story.**

_____

_____

Words That Compare

Most words that compare things end in **er** or **est**.
<u>Faster</u> and <u>fastest</u> are comparing words.

Use the er ending to compare two things.
Riding the bus is a <u>faster</u> way of getting to school than walking.

Use the est ending to compare more than two things.
Having your mom drive you is the <u>fastest</u> way of all.

▶ **Make comparing words by adding er and est. Then read each word aloud. The first one is done for you.**

1 strong   strong<u>er</u>   strong<u>est</u>

2 new   new_____   new_____

3 short   short_____   short_____

4 young   young_____   young_____

▶ **Write the correct word to complete each sentence.**

1 Our computer is _____ than our TV.
(newer/newest)

2 Dad is the _____ one in our family.
(older/oldest)

3 Mom is much _____ than I am.
(taller/tallest)

4 Our dog, Ruffy, is _____ of all.
(louder/loudest)

Final Blends

Many words end with two consonants. Their sounds blend together, but each sound is heard. In this story, you read many words that ended with blends.

desk   found   stamp   sent   find

▶ **Circle the consonant blend at the end of each word in the box.**

jump	went	lamp
sound	hand	found

▶ **Use the words from the word box to finish the sentences.**

1 Nana turned on a _____ after dark.

2 Nana and I heard a _____ outside.

3 The noise made me _____ up.

4 Nana and I _____ to the door.

5 Guess who we _____ at the door?

6 Dad had a pizza in his _____!

▶ **Write a sentence using two words from the box.**

_____

_____

Words to Learn

office	computer	e-mail	scan

▶ **Read the words in the box. Write the word that answers each riddle.**

1 I move fast from one computer to another. What am I?

_____

2 I am a room that has a desk and a computer. What am I?

_____

3 I am a machine that does many things. What am I?

_____

4 You do this when you want to copy a picture onto a computer. What do you do?

_____

▶ **Write the correct word to finish the sentences.**

Nana got herself a new _____ at the store. She set it up on the desk in her _____. Today she sent me an _____ from her computer to ours. I read her funny _____. Now Nana and I send _____ every day. Sometimes I will _____ pictures into my computer and send them to her. Nana's new _____ makes her very happy.

Reread

Quotation marks come before and after what someone says. When you see quotation marks, you know that someone is speaking. Make sure to read so that you sound like the character.

▶ Underline the words that are said in the passage below. With a partner, take turns reading this part of the story aloud. Use your voice to show what each sentence means.

Together, Nana and I wrote an e-mail to Tyson. When we finished, Nana said, "Now let's send some pictures."

I scanned the pictures into the computer and they popped up on the computer screen. I showed her how to attach the pictures to the e-mail. "Now click the SEND button," I said. She did, and the e-mail was sent.

"Well!" said Nana. "That was easy!" Nana smiled. "How long will it take?" she asked.

"Not long," I said. Then Nana wanted to send the pictures to Uncle Fred, too.

Nana finished the e-mail to Uncle Fred and attached the pictures herself. "This is so simple," Nana said. "I wish I had learned this sooner!"

Extend and Write

▶ What do you think Ella might write in her next e-mail to Nana? First, write your ideas. Then, write the e-mail.

ideas

To: _____

From: _____

Get Ready to Read
Wonderful Whales

1 Topic

whales

2 Words to Learn

mammal an animal that feeds milk to its young

blowhole a hole for breathing at the top of a whale's head

spout water that shoots up from a whale's blowhole

migrate move from one place to another when weather changes

whistle make a high, clear sound by forcing out air

3 Building Background

Why do people like whales?

Wonderful Whales

Kinds of Whales

Over 70 kinds of whales live in the ocean. Some live in rivers and smaller seas, too. They come in many sizes and shapes. Some are long and thin. Others are big and round. Most whales are white, black, or gray. They may have spots, lines, and other marks.

Some whales are only 4 feet long. Others can be as long as 100 feet. That's as big as a giant jet. Blue whales are the world's largest animals.

Blue whale

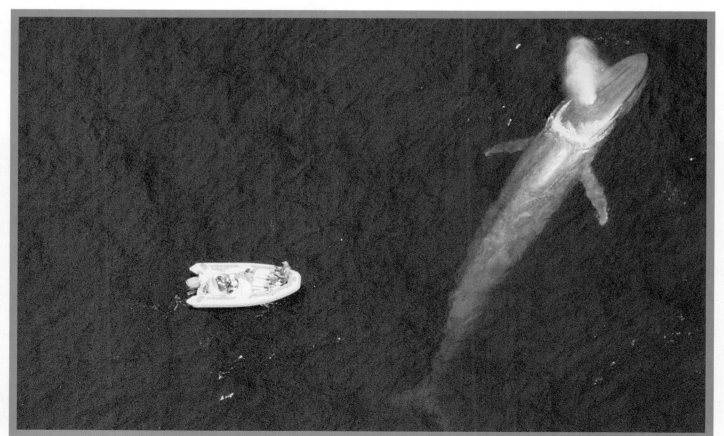

Sea Mammals

Whales can swim. They look a lot like fish. But whales are not fish. They are **mammals**, like dogs, horses, and people.

Whales swim by moving their tail up and down. They can swim fast. They can dive deep. Some whales can go down into the water more than a mile. They can stay under the water for a long time. But whales have to come up for air.

All mammals need air.

How do whales take in air? All whales have one or two **blowholes**. These holes are on the top of their head. Whales get air through their blowholes.

Whales also blow air out of their blowholes. Water sprays up with this air. You can see a water **spout** when the whale comes up. Each kind of whale has a different spout.

Ocean Trips

Many whales **migrate** in winter. They move from one feeding spot to another. These ocean trips can be up to 5,000 miles long. Most trips are much shorter.

Why do whales migrate?

Whale spout

Smart Whales

Whales live in groups. These groups help keep them safe. Together they watch the young whales. They drive off sharks.

Whales are smart. They have their own kind of "whale talk." They make many sounds. Some sounds are high. Others are low. Many whales can **whistle**. Some whales even make up whale songs. People believe that the whales use these songs to talk each other.

How do whales take care of young whales?

Living in groups keeps whales safer.

People and Whales

Today, people are trying to learn more about whales. They still have many questions. How do whales live? How smart are they? What do their songs mean? Many people love to study these interesting ocean mammals.

Some people take boat rides to see whales. They visit whales' feeding spots. With some luck, they will see many whales. They will see some whale spouts. They may even get to watch a whale leaping into the air.

Many people go on whale watches.

Classifying

Making groups of words that all tell about something can help you remember what you read.

▶ You read many things about whales in this article. Circle the words in the box that tell about whales.

long	silly	migrate	big	leap
small	white	red	black	gray
whistle	lazy	dive	shout	swim

▶ Write the words you circled in the box to complete each group.

How whales look

_____   _____

_____   _____

_____

What whales do

_____   _____

_____   _____

_____

Summarizing

A summary tells the most important parts of an article.

▶ **Put a T if the sentence is true. Cross out the sentences without a T.**

_____ Whales have blowholes on their tail.

_____ Whales look like fish, but they are mammals.

_____ Whales do not breathe air.

_____ Whales are the smallest animals in the ocean.

_____ Whales live in groups.

_____ Whales make many sounds to talk to each other.

▶ **Write a summary about whales. Use the true sentences to help you.**

_____

_____

_____

_____

_____

Words with Two Meanings

Many words have more than one meaning. Which meaning of <u>drive</u> is used in this sentence?

Whales <u>drive</u> sharks away.
- carry someone in a car
- chase something

board
- get on
- piece of wood

cold
- chilly, not warm
- sickness with a runny nose

waves
- moves a hand in the air
- rolling, moving water

rolls
- moves back and forth
- small, round kinds of bread

▶ **Write the correct meaning of each underlined word from the box above.**

1 We <u>board</u> a ship for a whale watch. _____

2 It is a <u>cold</u>, windy day. _____

3 The <u>waves</u> are big and fast. _____

4 The ship <u>rolls</u> in the waves. _____

Beginning Digraphs

Two consonants together that make one sound are called a digraph. A beginning digraph comes at the beginning of the word. Many words in the article begin with two consonants that make one sound: <u>wh</u>ale and <u>wh</u>ite, <u>sh</u>ip and <u>sh</u>ark, <u>th</u>ey and <u>th</u>an.

▶ **Make words by writing wh, sh, or th on each line. Then say each word.**

__wh__ istle	_____eir	_____arks
_____apes	_____ales	_____ese

▶ **Write the words from the box to finish the sentences.**

1 Blue _____ are the largest animals in the world.

2 _____ animals are very smart.

3 They _____ to speak to each other.

4 The older whales watch out for _____.

5 They get air through _____ blowholes.

6 Whales come in all different _____ and sizes.

Words to Learn

mammal	spout	blowhole
whistle	migrate	

▶ **Read the clues below. Find a word in the word box to answer each clue. Use your answers to finish the puzzle.**

Across

1 breathing hole on top of a whale's head

2 water that shoots up from a whale's blowhole

3 animal that feeds milk to its young

Down

4 move from one place to another

5 make a high, clear sound by forcing out air

Reread

> Before reading something out loud, look for any hard words. Practice those words. When you know how to say them, read the whole passage out loud.

Practice any hard words in the passage below. Then take turns with a partner reading the passage out loud.

Whales can swim. They look a lot like fish. But whales are not fish. They are mammals, like dogs, horses, and people.

Whales swim by moving their tail up and down. They can swim fast. They can dive deep. Some whales can go down more than a mile. They can stay under the water for a long time. But whales have to come up for air.

How do whales take in air? All whales have one or two blowholes. These holes are on the top of their head. Whales get air through their blowholes.

Extend and Write

▶ Imagine you went on a boat to see whales.
First, list some whale words. Then, write
what you saw during the whale watch on
the diary page below.

ideas

_____

_____

_____

_____

Grand Canyon

The Grand Canyon is a special place to visit. It is in Arizona. The Colorado River helped form the canyon. As the river flowed, it carved the canyon out of the rocks. The river flows for 277 miles through the canyon. If the river were a highway, it would take you more than four hours to drive from one end of the canyon to the other! The deepest point is 6,000 feet from top to bottom.

It takes people two days to hike on trails to the bottom of the canyon and back. Some people ride mules into the canyon. Others enjoy the view from high above. Each year, many people visit the Grand Canyon. They come to enjoy the beautiful colors, the deep canyon, and the powerful river.

▶ **Answer the questions below. Fill in the circle next to the best answer.**

1 What is the main idea of "Grand Canyon"?

Ⓐ The river flows for 277 miles through the canyon.

Ⓑ The Grand Canyon is a special place to visit.

Ⓒ Some people ride mules into the canyon.

Ⓓ The deepest point is 6,000 feet from the top of the wall to the floor.

2 What is one way people can get to the bottom of the canyon?

(A) People can drive a car to the bottom.

(B) People can ride bikes down to the bottom.

(C) People can take an elevator to the bottom.

(D) People can hike to the bottom.

3 What does **powerful** mean?

(A) strong

(B) weak

(C) colorful

(D) deep

4 Which word has the same vowel sound as **deep**?

(A) pet

(B) head

(C) meals

(D) bend

5 Which word completes this sentence?
At its _____ point, the Grand Canyon is 6,000 feet deep.

(A) deeper

(B) deepest

(C) longer

(D) longest

Glossary

Bb

blowhole a hole for breathing at the top of a whale's head

bulldozers big tractors that dig and move dirt

Cc

checkup when a vet checks an animal to see if it is healthy

coil to turn a rope in a circle

computer a machine that people use to do many jobs, such as writing letters

conductor a person who works on a train

cure to make feel better

Dd

dens homes under the ground where some animals live

derby a race

display to show off paintings or drawings

dye to add bright colors to something

Ee

e-mail a letter sent from one computer to another

excited happy that something is happening

Gg

gnaw chew

groundhogs small animals that dig holes and sleep through most of the winter

Ii

injured hurt

Mm

mammal an animal with warm blood that feeds milk to its young

market a place where things are sold

migrate move from one place to another when weather changes

model a small copy of a car

Oo

octopus a sea animal with eight arms

office a room with a desk and a computer where work is done

Pp

parade an event where people gather to watch other people march down a street

practice to do something many times

Rr

ramp a slanted piece of wood

Ss

scan to copy a picture onto a computer

sew to tie together with a needle and thread

spout water that shoots up from a whale's blowhole

startled scared by something

Tt

tradition something that has been passed down from parents to children

Vv

vet a doctor for animals

Ww

whistle make a high clear sound by forcing out air

workshop a place with tools to build and fix things